GONORRHEA

TAMRA ORR

ROSEN
PUBLISHING®

New York

Published in 2016 by The Rosen Publishing Group, Inc.
29 East 21st Street, New York, NY 10010

First Edition

Library of Congress Cataloging-in-Publication Data

Orr, Tamra.
Gonorrhea/Tamra B. Orr.
pages cm.—(Your sexual health)
Includes bibliographical references and index.
ISBN 978-1-4994-6058-2 (library bound)—ISBN 978-1-4994-6059-9 (pbk.)—ISBN 978-1-4994-6060-5 (6-pack)
1. Gonorrhea—Popular works. I. Title.
RC202.O77 2016
614.5'478—dc23

                                                                    2014042687

For many of the images in this book, the people photographed are models. The depictions do not imply actual situations or events

Manufactured in the United States of America

CONTENTS

Everything in life has risk. There is risk when you climb into the car to run to the grocery store. There is risk when you decide to learn a new sport that has you jumping, running, or moving in ways you have never done before. There is risk in falling in love—and there is definitely risk in having sex. All of those risks do not stop us from these activities, but just like you know to put on your seatbelt when you get in the car, knowing about sexually transmitted infections, or STIs, means you can take extra precautions to stay safe.

Gonorrhea is one of the oldest known types of STIs in history. The good news is that, over the centuries, the bacteria have become less potent, and while gonorrhea was once untreatable, today it is completely curable. The bad news is that curing it is becoming more challenging because of people's increasing use of antibiotics, which makes them more resistant to the effects of antibiotics that could treat gonorrhea. The bacterium that causes gonorrhea is incredibly complex and, as some physicians have said, very

Putting on a condom is like wearing a bike helmet. It is quick and easy, and it helps keep you safe. In some instances, it might even save your life.

"smart." Once treated by a certain type of antibiotic, the gonorrhea bacteria will not respond to it again. The rate of gonorrhea dropped dramatically between 1975 and 1997, hitting a record low in 2009. However, since then, it has slowly begun to rise again.

Having an STI like gonorrhea isn't like getting a cold or the flu. It doesn't just go away after a few days and life returns to normal. The symptoms of gonorrhea make a stuffy nose and sore throat seem pale in comparison. Most symptoms—if and when they appear—target the genitalia on both males and females. Left untreated, gonorrhea can complicate becoming pregnant or maintaining a pregnancy. The infection can also spread to other areas of the body, including the heart valves or the lining of the brain and spinal cord.

Getting gonorrhea is far from the end of the world. It happens to many people, and again, it is curable. In other words, suspecting that you have "the clap" (a common name for gonorrhea) isn't cause to go into hiding. It is a good reason to get yourself to the doctor, get tested, get treated, and get in touch with any sexual partners you have had. Even if you are not sexually active now, but you plan to be someday, learning to take precautions that can prevent an STI or what steps to take if you get an STI is important. This resource will help you understand what gonorrhea is, identify how to protect yourself from getting it, and recognize the symptoms of gonorrhea in the event that the precautions didn't work or were not used. It will take all the mystery—and fear—out of getting tested and getting treated. It will dispel a few myths, provide some resources, and hopefully give you peace of mind for whatever happens.

Throughout the resource, the acronym STI is most often used. The acronym STD (which stands for "sexually transmitted disease") is used either in quotes or in reference to published data by an individual or organization that still uses the older term.

Learning about STIs is part of becoming an adult. As you take responsibility for your risks, including having sex, you become a stronger, wiser, and more mature person. Always fasten that seatbelt—and read on.

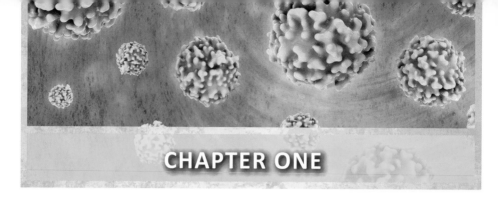

CHAPTER ONE

"The Flow of Seed"

No one can look back in time, point a finger at some poor person, and say, "THERE! This is the first case of gonorrhea! Blame it on this guy!" While no one is sure where the disease first started, researchers do know that gonorrhea is one of the oldest STIs. How far back it goes depends on which expert is asked and which study is done. Some say that it goes all the way back to ancient Chinese and Middle Eastern cultures in 3500 BCE. Records from that time period mention a disease that sounds a great deal like gonorrhea. Chinese emperor Huang Ti in 2600 BCE described a condition that resembled gonorrhea. Even the Old Testament in the Bible says, "Any man hath a running issue out of his flesh, because of this issue he is unclean" (Leviticus).

The disease finally got a name when the Greek physician Galen (130–200 CE) put together the Greek words for "semen" (*gonos*) and "to flow" (*rhoia*) to create the name "gonorrhea."

In 1161, the English Parliament was aware enough of gonorrhea to enact a law to try and reduce the spread of infection. They referred to the condition as "the perilous infirmity of burning." One hundred years later, France passed laws that banished anyone with the disease.

Historically, war and the rampant spread of STIs often go together. Some sources indicate

This poster from 1945 was designed to warn anyone in the armed forces about the health dangers associated with prostitution.

that ancient Roman soldiers who fought alongside Julius Caesar had gonorrhea. During the Crimean War of 1853–1856 (a conflict that pitted Russia against France, Britain, the Ottoman Empire, and Sardinia), STIs killed as many people as did malnutrition and other diseases put together. During World War I (1914–1918), the U.S. army discharged more than ten thousand soldiers due to STIs. Only the devastating flu pandemic of 1918–1919 resulted in more lost duty days than STIs during the war.

During World War II (1939–1945), posters were used to warn soldiers about the danger of spending time with "good time" girls or "procurable women" (i.e., prostitutes). Posters reminded the men, "You can't beat the Axis if you get VD [venereal disease]" and "Fool the Axis—Use Prophylaxis [protection]." Military men were lectured and shown movies about the dangers of getting an STI from prostitutes, and condoms were doled out daily.

NEISSER'S DISCOVERY

A German venereologist—a doctor who specializes in studying and treating sexually transmitted diseases—named Albert Ludwig Sigesmund Neisser (1855–1916) was the first person to identify the bacteria responsible for gonorrhea. For that, he was given the honor of having the bacteria named after him—*Neisseria*

"THE CLAP"

Like many health conditions, gonorrhea has gotten a number of nicknames over the years. It is known as "a dose," "GC," "a drip," and most commonly, "the clap." How does an STI get such a strange name? There are many different theories. One theory is that someone with gonorrhea experienced a "clapping sensation" whenever he or she had to urinate. Another theory states that the nickname came from a rough and fortunately outdated medical treatment of clapping an infected penis on both sides with a big, hardback book in order to remove pus. Ouch! Yet another theory is that the word came from the French word for brothels, *la clapiers*, because the men who visited these spots often ended up with gonorrhea. Other historians think that the word came from the French term *clapoir*, which was a late-sixteenth-century word for a sexual sore. A final theory is since many of the soldiers in World War I developed gonorrhea, they were often in for treatment. The medical personnel referred to the condition as "the collapse." Over time, it was shortened to "the clap."

gonorrhoeae. In 1879, when Neisser was twenty-four, he published his first paper, explaining how he had identified what he called "micrococci" in the smears taken from thirty-four subjects and how they specifically resulted in gonorrhea. In his later life, Neisser tried to find the causative agent for another STI, syphilis. He dedicated his life to advocating for public health and the prevention of STIs. In the article "Albert L. Neisser (1855–1916), Microbiologist and Venerologist," author Thomas G. Benedek states that Neisser spoke out against the prevailing attitude that prostitutes were to be blamed for the spread of gonorrhea, stating in 1890, "Much more is achieved when one recognizes that one is always dealing with sick people, sick not only in the physical, but frequently also in the psychological sense, and very frequently with people who are not automatically detestable, but rather are to be pitied and in need of help." In addition, he worked to educate the public about STIs and urged health agencies to make educating the public a priority. "With

Albert Neisser worked as hard at changing people's opinions as he did pinpointing the cause of STIs like gonorrhea and syphilis.

the enormous distribution of the disease and its severe complications," Benedek reports Neisser said in a presentation, "everyone must feel that it is high time to sound a warning on the matter. Gonorrhea is a social danger for the people and requires the most careful attention for the authorities who are responsible for the public health."

FROM PEPPERS TO PILLS

Like most diseases, the treatment for gonorrhea has improved greatly since it was first identified. An article on the Planned Parenthood website describes early treatments that were ineffective and often caused greater harm. In ancient Greece, the condition was treated with cold baths and vinegar. During the Middle Ages, Persian patients had to sleep in a cool bed with a metal plate across their genitals. Treatments in medieval England used injections of almond milk, breast milk, sugar, and violet oil.

Later, doctors tried using "cubebs," a type of Indonesian pepper. The dried powder of the pepper was mixed with licorice to help with the taste. This treatment did nothing to cure gonorrhea. It also caused a great deal of gastrointestinal disturbance, making the problem even worse. Another treatment was turpentine—also toxic and unhelpful. History also reports that some physicians used injections of mercury or silver nitrate directly into the penis. Other

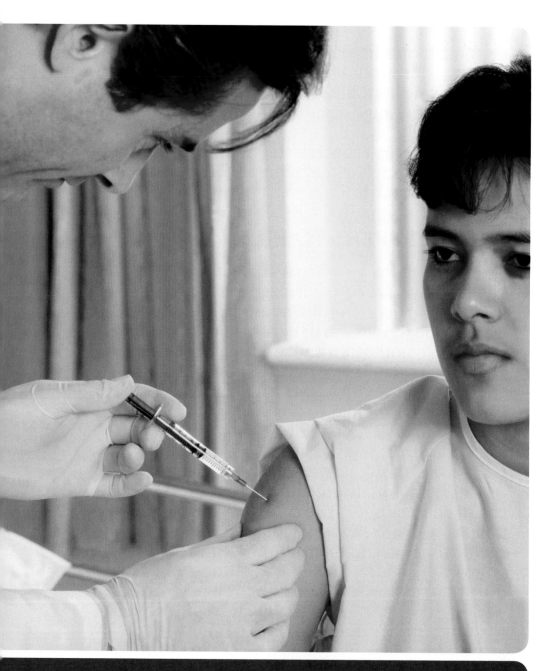

While no one enjoys getting a shot, it is certainly an easier way to get medical treatment than many of those used in the past.

attempted medications for the condition included arsenic or even gold.

Once Neisser identified the bacteria that gonorrhea came from, the race was on to create a vaccine from it. America's first vaccine was produced in 1910. Unfortunately, it did not work. The next attempt to cure gonorrhea was the use of a "fever cabinet." Similar in appearance to today's tanning beds, these cabinets enclosed all but a patient's head. Inside the cabinet, the temperature was kept at 110 degrees Fahrenheit (43 degrees Celsius). For ten hours the patient endured the heat, which doctors thought would "burn" the disease out of them. Doctors also used hyper-heated instruments on the genitalia, which was both painful and dangerous.

It was not until the 1940s that antibiotics were used against gonorrhea. At last, something helped. In fact, the antibiotics did such a good job that some people thought gonorrhea was soon going to be eradicated. Dr. John Mahoney from the U.S Public Health Service wrote in 1949, "As a result of antibiotic therapy, gonorrhea has almost passed from the scene as an important clinical and public entity."

Unfortunately, Dr. Mahoney and other medical professionals did not anticipate the gonorrhea bacteria's ability to adapt and thrive. It quickly became resistant to the initial type of antibiotics, and different antibiotics had to be used. This is a problem that has only grown. In late 2013, the Centers for Disease Control and Prevention

(CDC) classified antibiotic-resistant gonorrhea an "urgent threat."

TODAY'S TRENDS

The news on gonorrhea today is both good and bad. The good news is that reported cases are at historically low levels. Dr. Robert Kirkcaldy, medical epidemiologist for the CDC's Division of STD Prevention, says, "From 1974 to 1997, the national gonorrhea rate declined 74 percent. The rate reached 98.1 cases per 100,000 people in 2009, the lowest rate since national rates began to be recorded in the early 1940s. Since 2009, the rate has increased slightly each year to 107.5 cases per 100,000 people in 2012," with people aged twenty to twenty-four reporting the greatest incidence of infection.

The bad news is that resistance to antibiotics is making cases of infection harder and harder to treat. Dr. Kirkcaldy adds, "The development of new antibiotics is not keeping pace with the speed at which the bacteria are developing resistance, so we are running out of antibiotic options. This bacterium will continue to develop resistance, so preventing the spread of this infection is critically important."

MYTHS AND FACTS

MYTH
You can catch gonorrhea from sharing a towel, sitting in a hot tub, or a toilet seat.

FACT
Gonorrhea can ONLY be transmitted by unprotected oral, vaginal, or anal sex. That's it. Period. It is absolutely impossible to get it from a hot tub, towel, or toilet seat.

MYTH
If gonorrhea is left untreated, it can eventually become syphilis.

FACT
Each STI is its own separate disease. Just like strep throat cannot turn into the stomach flu, gonorrhea cannot turn into another type of STI, including syphilis. That said, it is possible to have two different STIs at the same time.

MYTH
You cannot get gonorrhea unless you sleep with multiple partners.

FACT
It takes having sex only one time with one infected partner to get gonorrhea. Your risk of getting any STI goes up with more partners, of course, because there is far more exposure. However, remember: it takes only one time and one person.

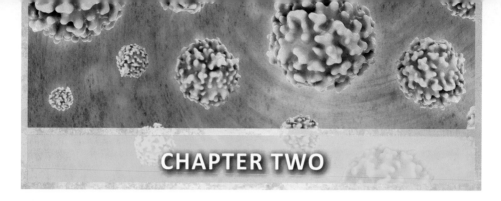

CHAPTER TWO

About *Neisseria Gonorrhoeae*

How does a person get gonorrhea? The fact that it is a sexually transmitted infection provides the biggest clue. It is possible for *Neisseria gonorrhoeae* to infect a person only if some sort of sexual activity is involved. You cannot get it from kissing. You cannot get it from sharing a bath or sharing a cup.

Simply put, gonorrhea is spread through sexual contact with the penis, vagina, mouth, or anus of an infected person. This means whatever type of sex a person is engaging in, including oral, vaginal, or anal sex, it carries a risk. The male does not have to ejaculate to pass on the infection. Because the bacterium is found in the semen and vaginal fluids, this means the disease can also be transmitted by sharing sexual toys that have not been cleaned. When infected body fluids come into contact with the body's mucous membranes, the bacterium thrives in the warm, moist reproductive tract. It settles in and begins to spread through a woman's cervix, uterus, and fallopian tubes

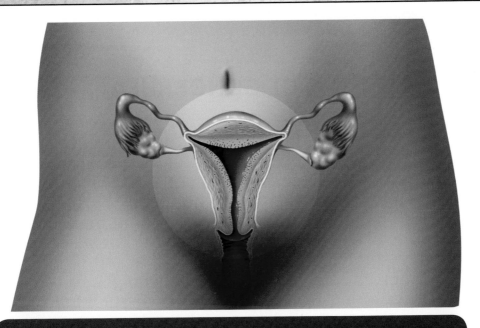

Each part of a female's reproductive system can be infected by gonorrhea. The infection can then move to other areas.

or a man's urethra. For those engaging in anal and oral sex, the bacteria may spread through the anus or the mouth and throat.

Anyone who has sex is susceptible to getting gonorrhea, but some people are at a higher risk than others. These include people who have had STIs in the past, those with multiple sexual partners, people who are sex workers, and drug users. According to the CDC, the southern region of the United States has the highest incidence of gonorrhea, followed by the Midwest, the Northeast, and then the West. The incidence of gonorrhea is highest in African Americans, but Hispanics have the fastest rate of increase based on statistics from 2010 to 2011.

SYMPTOMS OF GONORRHEA

STIs used to be called STDs. Why the change in terms? In STD, the "d" stands for disease, while the "i" in STI stands for infection. Medically speaking, an infection becomes a disease only when there are symptoms, and many of the STIs do not cause any obvious symptoms. That is one of the biggest problems with them—and with gonorrhea. Approximately four out of five women and one out of ten men who get gonorrhea either have no symptoms or such mild ones that they don't notice them. Many women

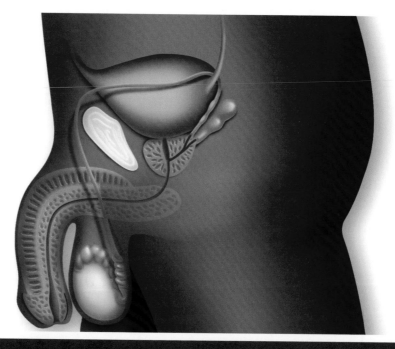

The male reproductive system tends to show symptoms of gonorrhea with more frequency than the female's, and symptoms also tend to appear more quickly than in females.

may notice the symptoms but assume they have a yeast infection and treat it with topical medication. Both genders might assume their fever and discomfort is nothing more than a case of the flu.

If you are sexually active, it is absolutely essential that you pay close attention to possible symptoms.

Symptoms typically begin as little as one to fourteen days after sex with an infected partner. In men, it is often a matter of a few days, but for women, it can take weeks to months for them to appear. Here are the signs to watch for:

For Males	For Females	For Both Genders
Greenish yellow/whitish discharge from penis or inside the penis	Abdominal or pelvic pain	Pain or burning when passing urine
Painful or swollen testicles	Vaginal discharge that is yellow or green and/or bloody	Fever
More frequent urination	Bleeding between menstrual periods	Itchy anus
	Heavy bleeding with periods	Anal discharge
	Pain during intercourse	Painful bowel movements
	Swelling or tenderness of the vulva	
	Vomiting	

LIVING WITH PID

Getting an STI isn't a pleasant experience, but most of the time it can be easily treated without lasting effects. Complications enter the picture, however, when STIs are left untreated. For women, an untreated STI, especially gonorrhea or chlamydia, can result in a far more serious condition called pelvic inflammatory disease, or PID. PID is an infection of a woman's reproductive organs. It is caused when the microorganisms from STIs move up from the cervix and vagina to the upper genital tract. PID can result in infertility and can permanently damage the reproductive organs. Statistics show that one out of five women with untreated gonorrhea will develop PID.

The symptoms of PID are often subtle and easy to overlook by both a young woman and her medical provider. The most common symptoms include:

- Lower abdominal pain
- Mild pelvic pain
- Increased vaginal discharge
- Irregular menstrual bleeding
- Fever
- Pain with intercourse
- Painful, frequent urination
- Abdominal tenderness
- Pelvic organ tenderness
- Uterine tenderness
- Cervical motion tenderness
- Inflammation

If **PID** is not treated, it can result in scarred fallopian tubes, pelvic adhesions, chronic pelvic pain, ectopic pregnancies, or infertility. While antibiotics can cure **PID**, they cannot reverse the scarring caused by the infection.

OTHER COMPLICATIONS

Mild symptoms can mislead some people into thinking that having gonorrhea is not a big problem. Nothing could be farther from the truth. Untreated gonorrhea can lead to serious and life-changing complications for both men and women.

For women, untreated gonorrhea can result in:

- Premature labor
- Stillbirth
- Ectopic pregnancy
- Blood, joint, and eye infections
- Pelvic inflammatory disease
- Infertility
- Increased risk of getting or spreading HIV
- Widespread infection to other parts of the body, including the blood, joints, or heart

While treating gonorrhea is generally effective, ignoring it can lead to more serious problems that cannot be reversed or cured.

For men, untreated gonorrhea can result in:

- Reduced fertility or sterility
- Painful inflammation of the testicles
- Epididymitis
- Urethral scarring
- Increased risk of getting or spreading HIV
- Widespread infection to other parts of the body, including the blood, joints, or heart

BABIES AND GONORRHEA

It is possible for a pregnant woman to get an STI, and in the case of gonorrhea, the infection can be passed to her baby during labor and delivery. Women who get gonorrhea while they are pregnant carry a higher risk of miscarriage. The baby's amniotic sac and the fluid in it can become infected. Preterm birth is a high risk.

The infection often affects the baby's eyes and can cause blindness if not treated. In most states, all babies are automatically treated with medicated eye drops soon after birth in case the mother has gonorrhea. In rare cases, the infection can also pass to other parts of the baby's body, resulting in blood or joint infections or meningitis, an inflammation of the membranes around the brain and the spinal cord.

Approximately three out of every one hundred people with untreated gonorrhea are at risk of developing disseminated gonococcal infection, or DGI. This condition causes arthritis (joint pain) and skin sores. It can be treated, but if it is not, it can permanently damage the joints of the body.

Getting infected with gonorrhea is silent; its symptoms can be, too. Unfortunately, this makes the infection far too easy to ignore, and the price for overlooking it can be very high. If you are sexually active, know what symptoms to watch for—and don't make the mistake of thinking it can't happen to you. It can.

CHAPTER THREE

Lowering the Risk, Preventing the Disease

I f you have sex, you run the risk of getting gonorrhea or another STI. But there are ways to lower your risk of infection and simple precautions you can take.

The most important key to preventing an STI is one you are already doing right now by reading this resource—you are getting educated. Knowing the risks, the symptoms, and the tests allows you to make wiser and more educated decisions regarding your sexual choices and your health.

ABSTINENCE

Abstinence is the best way to prevent an STI, but it is not necessarily an easy choice. You may feel pressured by friends or your partner to engage in some kind of sexual activity, or you may just be very eager to do so.

It often seems like "everyone is doing it," mostly because of the way that sex is portrayed in the media. However, research says that isn't quite true. An increasing number of teens are choosing not to have sex. According to the CDC, in 2002, abstinence in young men between fifteen and twenty-five years old was 5 percent. By 2008, that number had risen to 27 percent. For young women of the same age, 22 percent were abstinent in 2002, and by 2008, the number had increased to 29 percent.

If abstinence is not what you choose, then you need to make wise choices to have safer sex.

DISCUSSION

Talk to your sexual partner. Find out if he or she has ever had any kind of STI or has been checked for them. Find out if your partner has had a lot of sexual partners before you. This is important to know. Unless both of you have been completely abstinent up until now, it is best that you both get tested. (You can consider going together.) Also make sure your partner is as educated as you are about STIs and how to prevent them. Remember that vaginal, oral, and anal sex all have high risk factors, so whatever the two of you do needs to be discussed.

It may seem like a difficult conversation, but an easy way to get started could be to say something like, "I really care about you and our relationship, so there is something I want both of us to do," or "Before we have sex, we need to discuss STIs and contraception."

Most people feel embarrassed to talk about sex, contraception, and STIs with their partner. But just remember how important the topic is for both of you to remain healthy. Approach STIs as a medical issue. You'd want to know if your partner had mono before you kissed because you don't want to get it, right? It is the same thing with an STI. Next, prepare what you are going to say before you start. Pretend you're in English class and write out an outline of the main points you want to be sure to cover.

Being adult enough to consider having sex with your partner also means being adult enough to take on the responsibility of discussing sexual issues and making wise decisions together.

Practice talking out loud in the mirror. Use a matter-of-fact tone of voice, not a shy one.

Make sure to choose a good time and place to talk. In between classes in the hallway is not a good choice. You need a quiet, private place to be together and talk honestly. Don't wait until you're already starting to have sex either.

Your sexual drive may make having a conversation at that time difficult for both of you.

MONOGAMY

If you are going to be sexually active, you decrease your chances of STIs by having sex with only one partner. Agreeing to do this is referred to as "mutual monogamy." It makes sense that the fewer people involved, the lower your risk of getting an STI. If you're having sex with multiple people, chances are your partners are, too, and suddenly, there are many people involved and one of them might have gonorrhea or another STI.

COMPLICATIONS

Drinking alcohol or using drugs lowers inhibitions and makes it more likely you will end up having unprotected or unintentional sex. Under the influence of alcohol or drugs, you are apt to make bad or hasty decisions. This is sometimes referred to as alcohol myopia. Studies have repeatedly shown that when people of any age drink, they make poorer decisions and take more risks.

PROTECTION

You may already know that if you are going to have sex, you have to take precautions to avoid an unwanted pregnancy. Those same steps need to be taken to avoid getting an STI. There are a number of choices, including dental dams, female condoms, and male condoms.

A dental dam is a small, thin, square piece of latex that is used during oral-vaginal or oral-anal sex. These dams come in a variety of sizes and flavors. They prevent STIs by keeping vaginal and anal fluids away from the mouth. Dams are frequently used with water-based lubricants, and like regular condoms, they are for one-time use only. They can be purchased online or from specialty adult shops. Some contraception clinics like Planned Parenthood and college student health services may offer them for free. Dental dams can also be made from regular

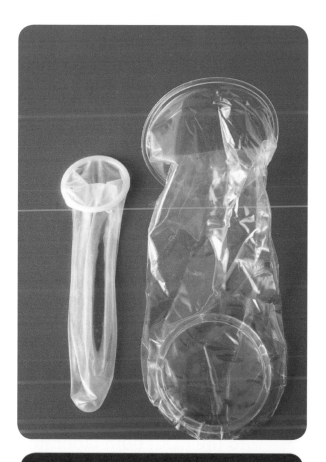

Male and female condoms shown from left to right. Condoms like these as well as dental dams are essential ways to protect yourself from STIs. Ask a doctor or school nurse for more information.

condoms by cutting off the tip and cutting down one side.

Female condoms are fairly new, and while not considered quite as effective at preventing STIs as the male condom, they are still recommended. A female condom is a pouch that is inserted into the vagina. It is made out of strong plastic called polyurethane or a substance called nitrile. It has flexible rings on each end. The ring at the closed end holds the pouch in place. The ring at the open end remains outside the vaginal opening during sex. For anal intercourse, the pouch is inserted into the anus.

Like male condoms, female condoms are generally found in drugstores and do not require a prescription. They can be used with oil- or water-based lubricants as well. They can be used during menstruation or pregnancy, and they can be inserted up to eight hours before sex. They should not be used, however, in conjunction with a male condom as the two can rub and cause discomfort or breakage.

Male condoms have been the main way to prevent STIs for decades. (Remember those war posters?) William Smith, the executive director for the National Coalition of STD Directors, says, "Please remember that condoms are the best tools in the toolbox for fighting gonorrhea. Condoms work really, really, really well." According to the CDC, both laboratory and epidemiologic studies have shown that latex condoms provide a truly effective barrier against even the tiniest

STI pathogens. Of course, their effectiveness relies completely on consistent and correct use, and users are constantly reminded to check condoms for holes or tears and to use a condom throughout the entire sex act, from initial sexual contact to ejaculation.

A study published in the *Archives of Pediatric and Adolescent Medicine* evaluated the relationship between consistent and correct condom use and gonorrhea infection. The study was based on more than five hundred sexually active adolescents between the ages of thirteen and nineteen. Their results were surprising even to them. The researchers reported that consistent and correct condom use resulted in a 90 percent reduction in the risk of gonorrhea! The overwhelming conclusion was "condoms remain the best STD and HIV prevention approach for persons whose sexual behaviors place them at risk for STDs." The researchers are not alone in advocating for using condoms. The United Nations Joint Programme on HIV/AIDS and the World Health Organization have both issued the same opinion.

Male condoms are usually made out of latex (hence the nickname "rubbers") or polyurethane. They vary in color, size, amount of lubrication and spermicide, and sometimes even flavor. Rolled over the erect penis, the condom prevents direct contact between the penis and vagina, so there is far less risk of contracting an STI. As every study has shown, using condoms is very effective for preventing infection. Using them properly is even more so, so make sure both you and your partner are educated about how to do it right.

Even with all of these precautions in place, the one rule that every health provider and organization has is, if you are sexually active, get tested for STIs regularly. It is simple, is inexpensive, and can keep you healthier while giving you, and your partner(s), peace of mind.

GETTING TESTED

How you are tested for gonorrhea depends largely on whom you go to for medical care. There are typically three types of tests that are used: swab, urine, and gram stain.

In the swab test, as the name indicates, a swab is taken of the urethra in men or the cervix in women. In the past, that is where the testing sites would have stopped. However, today, swabs are also often taken in the throat (for those who have had oral sex), the eye, and the rectum (for those who have had anal sex). Swab samples are sent to a lab where cultures—tests that place the sample in a prepared nutrient—are done to see what type of bacteria grow. These tests not only determine if there are any other STIs present but also can help pinpoint which antibiotics will treat the condition best. The swab test is the slowest; results typically take forty-eight to seventy-two hours.

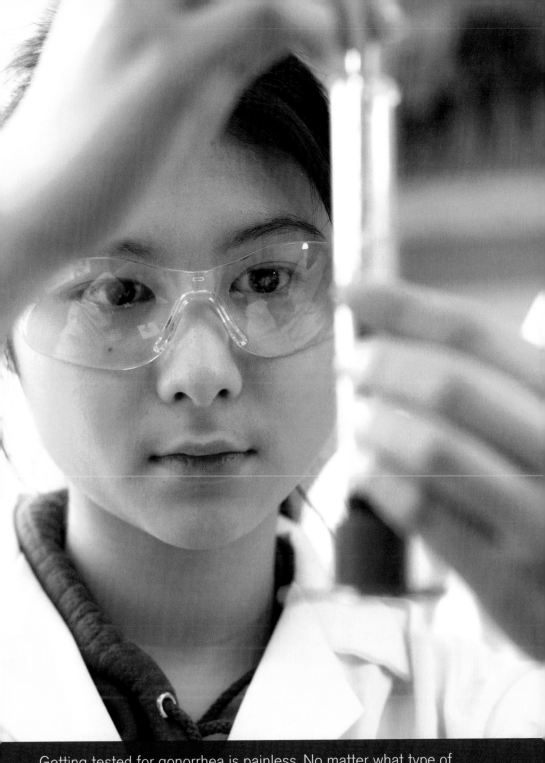

Getting tested for gonorrhea is painless. No matter what type of test is performed, it just requires a swab or a urine sample. Results are quick. Peace of mind is priceless.

The gram stain test also takes a swab of the urethra or the cervix, and then the sample is stained with a specific dye that makes the *Neisseria gonorrhoeae* bacteria easy to spot under a microscope. This is the fastest test, but it is not considered as accurate, and many doctor's offices do not have the equipment with which to perform the test.

The urine test requires a urine sample to analyze. It tends to be the most expensive of the tests, but it is very accurate and results are usually available the same day.

Most health care providers recommend you get screened annually for gonorrhea if you are a sexually active female under age twenty-five or if you are a man who has had sex with another man. Dr. Jeffrey Klausner, professor of medicine in the Division of Infectious Diseases and the Program in Global Health, adds, "Be sure if you get treated that your partner does too because these infections ping pong back and forth." He emphasizes that anyone who has had more than two sexual partners in the last year automatically get checked for a STI. He reminds young people that most school or sports checkups will not ask about sexual activity, so it is essential that students speak up. Say, "By the way, I am sexually active, so what should I be concerned about? Is there anything I should be tested for?"

Bringing up a topic like this can be uncomfortable, but it is still necessary. "In Northern

MANDATED REPORTING

Certain diseases are considered to be of significant importance to the general public's health. These diseases must be reported by law to the U.S. Centers for Disease Control and Prevention (CDC) by the health care provider either via a written report or a telephone call. The list of diseases is long and includes everything from anthrax and hepatitis to rabies and yellow fever. Gonorrhea, along with other STIs, is on this list.

According to the National Institutes of Health, getting these numbers helps researchers "identify disease trends and track disease outbreaks." In the case of STIs, the county or state may also try to locate sexual contacts of infected people to ensure they are disease-free or get the treatment they need if already infected.

Europe," adds Klausner, "There are adolescent friendly clinics for STIs, contraception, and sexual issues, so kids don't have to go to their primary doctor. Unfortunately, here, we just defund these types of programs."

In recent years, home tests for gonorrhea have become available via the Internet. For men, it is usually as simple as sending in a urine sample to be tested in the company's lab. For women, the tests usually require a swab. Companies provide prepaid envelopes for sending in the samples, and results arrive in the mail in two to ten days.

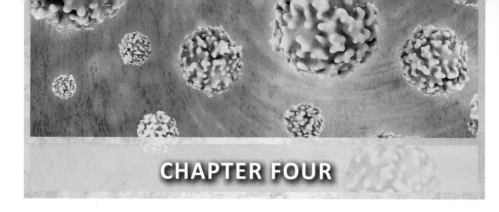

CHAPTER FOUR

When the Test Is Positive

A positive test result may make you cry, rage, moan, complain, and sigh. Just remember to also talk things through with an adult and make wise decisions for treatment.

I f you are tested for gonorrhea and the results are positive, it won't make your day, of course, but don't let it break your day either. Remember, gonorrhea is a common disease, and it is completely curable. The first thing you need to do is get treatment. Talking to your parents or a trusted adult is a good idea. They can help make sure you get to the doctor and get proper medical care. They also love you and are likely to support you in making the best decisions.

Talking to an adult or medical professional about your diagnosis is only one of the conversations you need to have. It is absolutely essential (and the right thing to do) to inform any of the anal, vaginal, or oral sex partners with whom you have had sex within sixty days of the first onset of symptoms and/or positive diagnosis. They deserve to know so that they, too, can get to the doctor and get checked and treated, if necessary.

Telling your partner that you have gonorrhea can feel even more awkward than having the STI conversation about whether he or she has been tested and how many partners he or she has had previously. The rules for how to initiate this conversation are almost the same, however. Pick a time and place where you can have privacy. Have your information lined up and ready, and don't make the announcement when you're in the middle of fooling around. (It's a definite mood killer.) Practice what you are going to say, explain what you have learned about treatment, and then listen patiently in return. Find a way to work through the situation together.

TAKING YOUR MEDICINE

The best treatment for gonorrhea is taking antibiotics. (Take a moment to be grateful that those days of turpentine doses or penile injections are long gone!) The type of antibiotics doctors

Your pharmacist is a great person to ask questions of when you are taking a new medication. You might want to ask if you should take your pills with or without food or at what time of day.

use has changed a number of times over the years. The first was sulfonamide in the 1930s and 1940s, followed by penicillin, tetracycline, spectinomycin, and then ceftriaxone. The type of antibiotic keeps changing because *Neisseria gonorrhoeae* is a sneaky bacterium. If gonorrhea was a villain, it would be one that would certainly exasperate most superheroes. It is clever—crafty even—with an amazing memory and an ability to resist every antibiotic treatment that is thrown at it. Just ask the CDC. It has had to change its recommendations for treatment three times: in 1985, 2007, and 2012. Currently, it recommends a combination of antibiotics to make sure they are effective. First, an injection of ceftriaxone is given, followed by either a single dose, by pill, of azithromycin or seven days of the drug doxycycline, which is also taken orally.

The rule with antibiotics is that you must take all of them, even if your symptoms have completely disappeared before you finish taking the full dose. It is important to realize, too, that while the antibiotics will cure the infection, they cannot repair any damage that the infection might have caused. Avoid having any type of sex with a partner until you have completed your treatment and no longer have any symptoms.

Because of the rising problem of antibiotic resistance, it is vital that if your symptoms do not go away entirely, you go back to your medical provider for further testing. You might be one of those people who have a very resistant strain of gonorrhea, and your doctor not only has to know that but needs to report it as a "treatment failure." You will most likely need a different type of antibiotic.

A positive test for gonorrhea is nothing to ignore, but neither is it a reason to panic. If you were mature enough to be sexually active, be mature enough to get the care and treatment you need to get past this—and stay healthy.

A LOOK TO THE FUTURE

William Smith is the executive director for the National Coalition of STD Directors, and he speaks often about the problem of antibiotic-resistance and gonorrhea. "Resistance is largely attributable to the overuse of antibiotics," he says. "Usually there are other drugs in the pipeline to use when people become resistant to a certain medication, but with gonorrhea," he adds, "we are at the edge of the cliff as there are virtually no other demonstrated or approved drugs to use. We need new ones."

"Gonorrhea is a really, really, really smart organism," he explains. "Once it develops resistance to an antibiotic, it carries that information in its DNA for its lifetime. It isn't going to forget it, and so treatment can't go back to using it. Not all organisms can do that—but gonorrhea can." The problem doesn't end there, however. According to Smith, no new classes of antibiotics are being created because drug companies are focusing far more on lifestyle drugs. "They make more money on the drugs that people have to take their entire lives, like medications for HIV, heart disease, or diabetes. There is little to be made on conditions that only require a single dose to treat, and these companies want a higher return on their investment."

Smith does see some hope for the future. "Gonorrhea treatment will see new drugs," he says, "but they will also be very expensive." Smith believes that President Obama's September 2014 executive order to take action to combat the rise of antibiotic-resistant bacteria is another step in the right direction. The new task force will make the development

Studying resistance by tracking patients and asking questions will hopefully lead experts to new answers and treatment possibilities.

and spread of antibiotic resistance a top national security and public health priority. Smith hopes that through this new program, medical providers will not only test for gonorrhea but will look further to determine the level of resistance in each individual and then choose the best medication. "Using the stronger medication on those with little resistance," he explains, "is like killing an ant with a sledgehammer when a fingertip would work. This would also prolong the life of the antibiotics we currently have and empower doctors to tailor treatment for patients."

10 GREAT QUESTIONS
TO ASK A MEDICAL PROFESSIONAL

1. What are the symptoms of gonorrhea?

2. What other conditions might be causing these symptoms?

3. How is gonorrhea transmitted?

4. Why types of testing do I need and what do they involve?

5. Will tests for other types of STIs be performed? Why or why not?

6. Should my past or current sexual partners also be tested?

7. What types of precautions should my partner(s) and I take while waiting for the test results?

8. When will the test results be available and should I call in or will someone call me?

9. If my partner tests negative for gonorrhea, how can I avoid spreading it to him/her?

10. Once the gonorrhea is gone, what do I need to do in order to make sure I do not get it again?

CHAPTER FIVE

Coping with Gonorrhea

Y ou can show maturity about your sexual health by initiating a conversation with your partner(s) about whether they have been tested and how many previous partners they have had. You also show maturity by making decisions about whom you choose to have sex with and what kinds of protection you use. However, getting an STI like gonorrhea can still make you feel socially stigmatized despite all of the choices you have made to show that you are a mature

It is essential to remember that gonorrhea, as with other STIs, can affect both genders, all ages, and all racial backgrounds. No one who is sexually active is immune.

and responsible person. Social stigmas—particularly about STIs—are judgments or condemnation by others largely because you can only get them from having sex. For some, anything having to do with sex may be looked down upon or criticized, despite the fact that most people are either going to have sex in the future, are currently having sex, or used to have sex in the past. This stigma can make you feel guilty or embarrassed, both for having sex

Figure 16. Gonorrhea — Rates of Reported Cases by Age and Sex, United States, 2013

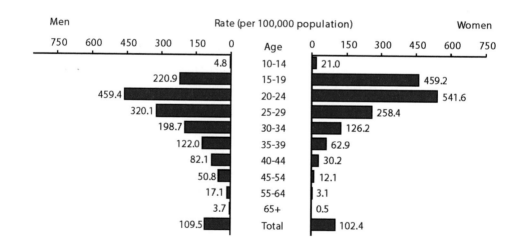

Men get gonorrhea at slightly higher rates than women except in the three youngest age groups.

and for contracting an STI. The fact is, your sexual health is only your concern and that of your partner(s). Contracting gonorrhea—or any other STI—does not make you a bad person.

An STI is an infection, just like the stomach flu or an inner ear infection. Infections cannot be moral or immoral. They affect everyone, male and female, young and old. Millions of people get them every year.

It takes having sex only with one person one time to get an STI. Having gonorrhea does not mean that you have a promiscuous sex life.

Gonorrhea often shows mild to no symptoms, so it is very easy to pass the infection on from one person to the next without knowing.

A LITTLE EXTRA HELP

Allowing yourself to feel embarrassed or guilty may get in the way of doing what you need to do—getting medical care. It can also make you feel stressed or depressed. If so, you need to take one more step—find someone to talk to. A parent, teacher, partner, or good friend is a great choice. Often they are the best people to talk with because they care about you and want to help you. Sometimes, however, that isn't possible or you might need more information or support than they are able to give you. The next step is to get some professional counseling.

A counselor can help you to deal with all kinds of emotional and physical challenges and

☤ TRANSLATING THE SCIENCE

Lynn Barclay, president and CEO of ASHA, the American Sexual Health Association, explains that they are all about translating science to the lay person. "We are talking to people, not medical providers." ASHA was the first sexual health organization in the United States, founded in 1914 in New York City. "At that time, syphilis and gonorrhea were rampant and no one knew why," says Barclay. Several prominent people, including actor Katherine Hepburn's father, got together and decided something should be done, and so the American Social Hygiene Association was formed. In 2012, the association renamed itself the American Sexual Health Association. "For decades, this group was the only one speaking out about what was then called VD, or venereal disease," adds Barclay. "Today the disease frame has improved in that there is less stigma and fear associated with STIs."

Because of this, ASHA's focus has changed to supporting sexual health. "We are not just about avoiding disease and unplanned pregnancies, but about how to feel good about yourself, and be in a healthy sexual relationship," continues Barclay. Her best advice to young people today, in addition to using ASHA's website for helpful information, is to talk to their parents. "They might not have all the answers, but they were young once, and can often help." According to Barclay, teens who talk to their parents about sexual questions and issues are far more likely to use safer sex practices.

can also help you come to terms with having an STI. Along with making sure you have the necessary information about your condition and helping you understand your treatment options, a good counselor will also talk to you about overcoming feelings of shame, as well as guide you in ways of safer sexual behavior for the future. He or she will likely take a comprehensive sexual history and then use a variety of methods for talking with you, including open-ended questions ("Tell me about your experience with using condoms . . .") and what is called "normalizing" language, or questions

Talking with others who are in the same situation or who have had an STI can be the key to accepting what is going on and knowing how to cope.

asked to remind you that other people have struggled with the same issues as you.

HELPING A FRIEND

If the person who is being treated for gonorrhea is someone you care about, such as a brother, sister, or friend, congratulations for caring enough about that person to learn about the disease and find ways to actively help. Supporting friends who have an STI is much like supporting them through other life challenges, from other illnesses or injuries to dealing with broken relationships or other kinds of disappointment. Here are a few suggestions of what you can do to help:

- Make sure your loved one realizes how important it is to get proper medical care and treatment.

FINDING SUPPORT AND UNDERSTANDING

One of the most important keys to coping with contracting the gonorrhea infection is making sure you have a strong support system in place. When you have people you can talk with honestly and without fear of judgment, it can make it easier to accept, make wise decisions, and follow through with recommended treatment.

In addition to turning to family and friends, there are also many support groups and organizations that can help. Going to a local group where everyone truly does know what you are going through can be empowering and comforting. You can search online for a local group, or check in with your doctor for contact information. Some helpful websites to check out include NPIN: National Prevention Information Network, WebMD's Sexually Transmitted Diseases Community, or MD Junction's STD Teens Online Support Group. There are even websites that help you date after dealing with an STI. Positive Singles is the number one community for STD dating and support. Links to some helpful organizations can be found at the end of this resource.

Please be aware that searching online for help may be appealing because you can remain anonymous, but the Internet also has a lot of misinformation. It is best to check with a medical professional about your diagnosis and treatment. Please also note that of the three websites mentioned above, only one of them is a teen support group. If you are under the age of eighteen, participating in group discussions may be inappropriate depending on the content of the discussion. Remember never to disclose any personal information online and to maintain a strict level of respect for yourself and any other participants.

- Make sure the person understands what gonorrhea is, how he or she got it, and how it can affect him or her if treatment is not pursued.
- Listen patiently when your loved one gets angry, depressed, frustrated, or embarrassed, and remember that there are a lot of emotions that may come to the surface for a person dealing with having an STI.
- Go with the person to the doctor or health clinic if he or she needs support or company.
- Encourage the person to let sexual partner(s) know about the diagnosis.
- Help find local support groups or a professional counselor.
- Observe your relative or friend carefully to see if he or she becomes depressed or exhibits any dangerous behavior.

Being a friend means being there for all the laughter and fun times—and all the rough spots as well. Your friendship and support during the testing and treatment of an STI can mean everything to someone. Whether you are the one dealing with gonorrhea, or you are the best friend who is stepping up to help, the key is education, awareness, and a positive attitude.

GLOSSARY

brothel A business/house when men can solicit prostitutes.

chlamydia A type of sexually transmitted disease.

dental dam A thin sheet of latex to use as a condom during oral and anal sex.

disseminated gonococcal infection Gonorrheal infection that spreads beyond the genitalia and causes arthritis.

ectopic pregnancy A pregnancy in which the embryo implants in the fallopian tubes instead of the uterus.

ejaculate The ejection of semen from a male body at the moment of sexual climax.

epidemiologist A person who specializes in studying the cause, distribution, and control of diseases.

epididymitis Inflammation of the coiled tubes in the back of the testicles.

female condom Contraceptive device that is inserted into a woman's vagina or anus before intercourse.

gastrointestinal Relating to the stomach and intestinal tract.

genitalia External reproductive organs.

lubricant A substance used for minimizing friction during sexual intercourse.

meningitis Inflammation of the brain lining caused by a viral or bacterial infection.

monogamy The practice of being with only one sexual partner at a time.

mucous membrane A tissue that secretes mucus and lines body cavities including the stomach and respiratory passages.

pandemic A disease that is prevalent over an entire country or world.

spermicide A substance that kills sperm and can be used as a contraceptive or with another contraceptive.

topical Applied to the skin.

urethra The duct by which urine is carried out of the body from the bladder; in males, it also conveys semen.

venereologist A person who specializes in studying sexually transmitted diseases.

FOR MORE INFORMATION

Advocates for Youth
2000 M Street NW, Suite 750
Washington, DC 20036
(202) 419-3420
Website: http://www.advocatesforyouth.org
The goal of Advocates for Youth is to help
    young people make informed and respon-
    sible decisions about their reproductive
    and sexual health.

American College Health Association
1362 Mellon Road, Suite 180
Hanover, MD 21076
(410) 859-1500
Website: http://www.acha.org
ACHA's mission is to advance the health of
    college students and campus communi-
    ties through advocacy, education, and
    research.

American Sexual Health Association (ASHA)
P.O. Box 13827
Research Triangle Park, NC 27709
(919) 361-8400
Website: http://www.ashasexualhealth.org
ASHA's goal is to improve the health of indi-
    viduals, families, and communities, and
    its main focus is on preventing STIs and
    their consequences.

Canadian Federation for Sexual Health
2197 Riverside Drive, Suite 403

Ottawa, ON K1H 7X3
Canada
(613) 241-4474
Website: http://www.cfsh.ca
The Canadian Federation for Sexual Health is
    dedicated to supporting access to comprehen-
    sive sexual and reproductive health
    education, information, and services.

Canadians for Choice
251 Bank Street, 2nd Floor
Ottawa, ON K2P 1X3
Canada
(613) 789-9958
Website: http://www.canadiansforchoice.ca
Canadians for Choice is dedicated to ensuring
    reproductive choice for all Canadians,
    including preventing unwanted pregnancies,
    promoting contraception, and educating
    women, men and youth.

WEBSITES

Because of the changing nature of Internet links,
Rosen Publishing has developed an online list of
websites related to the subject of this book. This
site is updated regularly. Please use this link to
access the list:

http://www.rosenlinks.com/YSH/Gon

FOR FURTHER READING

Axolotl Academic Publishing. *Sex Ed: A Sexual Health Primer for Teens and Young Adults.* Louisville, KY: Axolotl Academic Publishing Co., 2012.

Carroll, Janell. *Sexuality Now: Embracing Diversity.* Florence, KY: Cengage Learning, 2012.

Collins, Nicholas. *Frequently Asked Questions About STDs.* New York, NY: Rosen Publishing, 2011.

D'Souza, Arthur. *Sexually Transmitted Diseases.* Seattle, WA: CreateSpace Independent Publishing, 2014.

Equin, Marvin. *The Truth About STDs.* Seattle, WA: Amazon Digital Services, 2012.

Fonda, Jane. *Being a Teen: Everything Teen Girls and Boys Should Know About Relationships, Sex, Love, Health, Identity, and More.* New York, NY: Random House, 2014.

Guddat, Gina. *Unwrapped: Real Questions Asked by Real Girls (About Sex).* Seattle, WA: Amazon Digital Services, 2011.

Handsfield, Hunter. *Color Atlas and Synopsis of Sexually Transmitted Diseases.* New York, NY: McGraw-Hill, 2011.

Henderson, Elisabeth. *100 Questions You'd Never Ask Your Parents: Straight Answers to Teens' Questions About Sex, Sexuality, and Health.* New York, NY: Roaring Brook Press, 2013.

Libby, Roger. *The Naked Truth About Sex: A Guide to Intelligent Sexual Choices for Teenagers and Twentysomethings.* Wilmington, DE: Freedom Press, 2013.

Magill, Elizabeth. *Sexual Health Information for Teens: Health Tips About Sexual Development, Reproduction, Contraception, and Sexually Transmitted Infections.* Ashton, PA: Omnigraphics, 2011.

Schalet, Amy. *Not Under My Roof: Parents, Teens, and the Culture of Sex.* Chicago, IL: University of Chicago Press, 2011.

Yancey, Diane. *STDs* (USA Today Health Reports: Diseases and Disorders). Minneapolis, MN: Twenty-First Century Books, 2011.

BIBLIOGRAPHY

Baby Center Medical Advisory Board. "Gonorrhea During Pregnancy." March 2013. Retrieved October 5, 2014 (http://www.babycenter.com).

Barclay, Lynn. Telephone interview by author, October 14, 2014.

Benedek, Thomas G. "Albert L. Neisser (1855–1916), Microbiolgist and Venerologist." AntiMicrobe.org. Retrieved October 3, 2014 (http://www.antimicrobe.org).

Boskey, Elizabeth, Ph.D. "How Do I Get Tested for Gonorrhea?" About Health, May 21, 2014. Retrieved October 6, 2014 (http://std.about.com).

Brown University Health Promotion. "Talking About STIs with a Partner." Retrieved October 5, 2014 (http://www.brown.edu).

BuzzFeed. "The 12 Best World War II STD Posters." Retrieved October 6, 2014 (http://www.buzzfeed.com).

Cates, Willard, Jr. "The NIH Condom Report: The Glass Is 90% Full." Guttmacher.org, September/October 2001. Retrieved October 11, 2014 (https://www.guttmacher.org).

Centers for Disease Control and Prevention. "Condom Effectiveness." Retrieved October 7, 2014 (http://www.cdc.gov).

Centers for Disease Control and Prevention. "Pelvic Inflammatory Disease (PID)–CDC Fact Sheet." Retrieved October 7, 2014 (http://www.cdc.gov/std/pid/stdfact-pid-detailed.htm).

Centers for Disease Control and Prevention.

"2011 Sexually Transmitted Diseases Surveillance: Gonorhea." Retrieved October 4, 2014 (http://www.cdc.gov).

Hamilton, Lee Ann, et al. "Sex Talk." University of Arizona Campus Health Service. Retrieved October 1, 2014 (https://www.health .arizona.edu).

Hiers, Mary. "The Fascinating History of the Government's Anti-STD Efforts." AccessRx, August 25, 2014. Retrieved October 8, 2014 (http://www.accessrx.com).

Kidd, Sarah, et al. "Cephalosporin-Resistant *Neisseria Gonorrhoeae* Public Health Response Plan." Centers for Disease Control, August 2012. Retrieved October 9, 2014 (http://www.cdc.gov).

Kirkaldy, Robert, MD. E-mail interview with author, October 14, 2014.

Klausner, Jeffrey, Ph.D. Telephone interview with author, October 7, 2014.

KnowsWhy.com. "Why Is Gonorrhea Called Clap?" Retrieved October 2, 2014 (http://www.knowswhy.com).

Mandal, Ananya, Ph.D. "Gonorrhea History." News Medical. Retrieved October 7, 2014 (http://www.news-medical.net/health/Gonorrhea-History.aspx).

Medline Plus. "Female Condoms." Retrieved October 6, 2014 (http://www.nlm.nih.gov/medlineplus/ency/article/004002.htm).

Medline Plus. "Reportable Diseases." Retrieved October 6, 2014 (http://www.nlm.nih.gov/

medlineplus/ency/article/001929.htm).

Mimalasuriya, Kshamica S., MD. "Stepping Up STI Counseling and Prevention." Medscape, July 20, 2011. Retrieved October 4, 2014 (http://www.medscape.com/viewarticle/746451_3).

Planned Parenthood. "Gonorrhea." Retrieved October 3, 2014 (http://www.plannedparenthood.org).

Smith, William. Telephone interview with author, October 10, 2014.

WebMD.com. "Gonorrhea—What Happens." Retrieved October 7, 2014 (http://www.webmd.com).

Wohlfeiler, Dan. E-mail interview with author, October 2, 2014.

WomensHealth.gov. "Gonorrhea Fact Sheet." Retrieved October 2, 2014 (http://www.womenshealth.gov).

INDEX

ABOUT THE AUTHOR

Tamra Orr is a full-time writer and author living in the Pacific Northwest. Orr graduated from Ball State University with a degree in English/secondary education and public health and safety. She is the author of a number of health-related books, including *When the Mirror Lies: Anorexia, Bulimia, and Other Eating Disorders, Amenorrhea, Frequently Asked Questions About Date Rape, Polio,* and *Ovarian Cysts and Tumors.* She is the mother of four young adults, all of whom she has made sure know all about STIs and how to avoid them.

PHOTO CREDITS

Designer: Michael Moy; Editor: Tracey Baptiste